DATE DUE

PRINTED IN U.S.A.

FAST FACT MATH

FAST FACT FRACTIONS

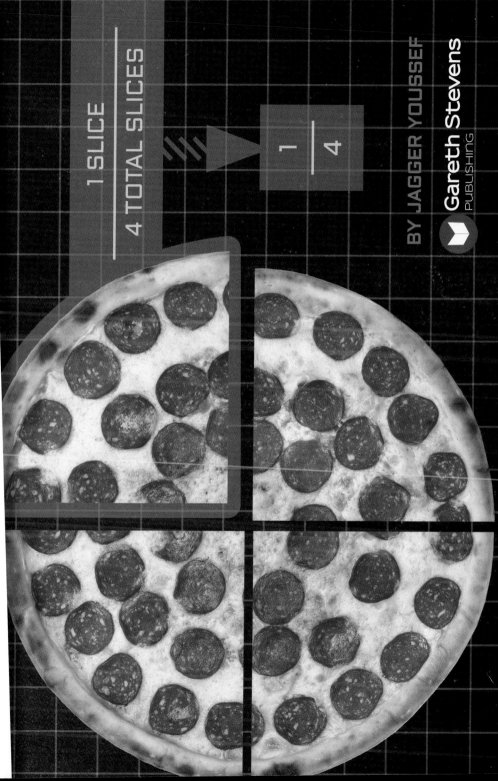

1 SLICE

4 TOTAL SLICES

$$\frac{1}{4}$$

BY JAGGER YOUSSEF

Gareth Stevens
PUBLISHING

Please visit our website, www.garethstevens.com. For a free color catalog of all our high-quality books, call toll free 1-800-542-2595 or fax 1-877-542-2596.

Cataloging-in-Publication Data

Names: Youssef, Jagger.
Title: Fast fact fractions / Jagger Youssef.
Description: New York : Gareth Stevens Publishing, 2019. | Series: Fast fact math |
Includes index.
Identifiers: LCCN ISBN 9781538219812 (pbk.) | ISBN 9781538219799 (library bound) | ISBN
9781538219829 (6 pack)
Subjects: LCSH: Fractions–Juvenile literature.
Classification: LCC QA117.Y68 2019 | DDC 513.26–dc23

First Edition

Published in 2019 by
Gareth Stevens Publishing
111 East 14th Street, Suite 349
New York, NY 10003

Designer: Sarah Liddell
Editor: Therese Shea

Photo credits: Cover, p. 1 Anna Mandrikyan/Shutterstock.com; chalkboard background used
throughout mexrix/Shutterstock.com; p. 5 Elena Hramova/Shutterstock.com; pp. 7, 10, 14 Evikka/
Shutterstock.com; p. 9 Artem Silionov/Shutterstock.com; p. 11 momemoment/Shutterstock.com;
p. 13 Gts/Shutterstock.com; p. 15 Kucher Serhii/Shutterstock.com; p. 17 (top left) jonson/
Shutterstock.com; p. 17 (top right) Idiaphoto/Shutterstock.com; p. 17 (bottom left) Westend61/
Shutterstock.com; p. 17 (bottom right) bergamont/Shutterstock.com; p. 19 IriGri/Shutterstock.com;
p. 20 Hogan Imaging/Shutterstock.com; p. 21 wavebreakmedia/Shutterstock.com.

Printed in the United States of America

CONTENTS

Words in the glossary appear in **bold** type the first time they are used in the text.

BREAKING IT DOWN

Fractions may look more **confusing** than whole numbers. However, they're not hard to understand. Picture a whole object separated into equal parts. One or more of those parts is a fraction of the whole object.

Understanding fractions becomes easier when you realize they're all around us. They're part of everyday life! This book will teach you some "fast facts" about fractions and show you how to recognize fractions in your life. Are you ready?

MATH MANIA!

As you read this book, you'll become a master **mathematician**. Get ready to use your fraction skills to figure out the problems in boxes like this. Look for the upside-down answers to check your work. Good luck!

FRACTIONS MAY REQUIRE A BIT OF IMAGINATION AT FIRST! YOU COULD MAKE MODELS LIKE THIS TO HELP YOU UNDERSTAND THEM.

FRACTION WORDS

NUMERATOR $\longrightarrow \dfrac{1}{4}$ $\longleftarrow$ DENOMINATOR

The denominator tells you the number of equal parts that make up the whole. The numerator **represents** a certain number of those parts.

The fraction $\dfrac{1}{4}$ stands for 1 part of a whole that has 4 equal parts. Pizza is a tasty way to picture this fraction! If you ate 1 piece of a pizza with 4 equal pieces, you ate $\dfrac{1}{4}$ of it.

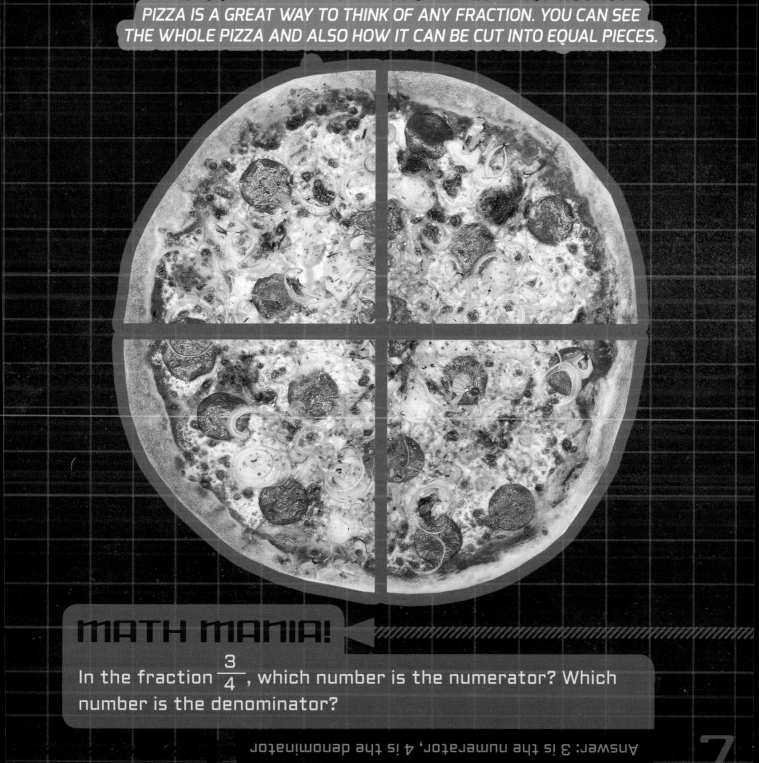

PIZZA IS A GREAT WAY TO THINK OF ANY FRACTION. YOU CAN SEE THE WHOLE PIZZA AND ALSO HOW IT CAN BE CUT INTO EQUAL PIECES.

MATH MANIA!

In the fraction $\frac{3}{4}$, which number is the numerator? Which number is the denominator?

IN BETWEEN

FAST FACT: A fraction is a number between two whole numbers.

It's easy to see this fast fact is true when you locate a fraction on a number line. The number line below shows where $\frac{1}{2}$ falls between 0 and 1. It's halfway between 0 and 1.

If you **divide** the line between 0 and 1 into thirds, you can see where $\frac{1}{3}$ and $\frac{2}{3}$ are located:

What fraction of the number line below is colored?

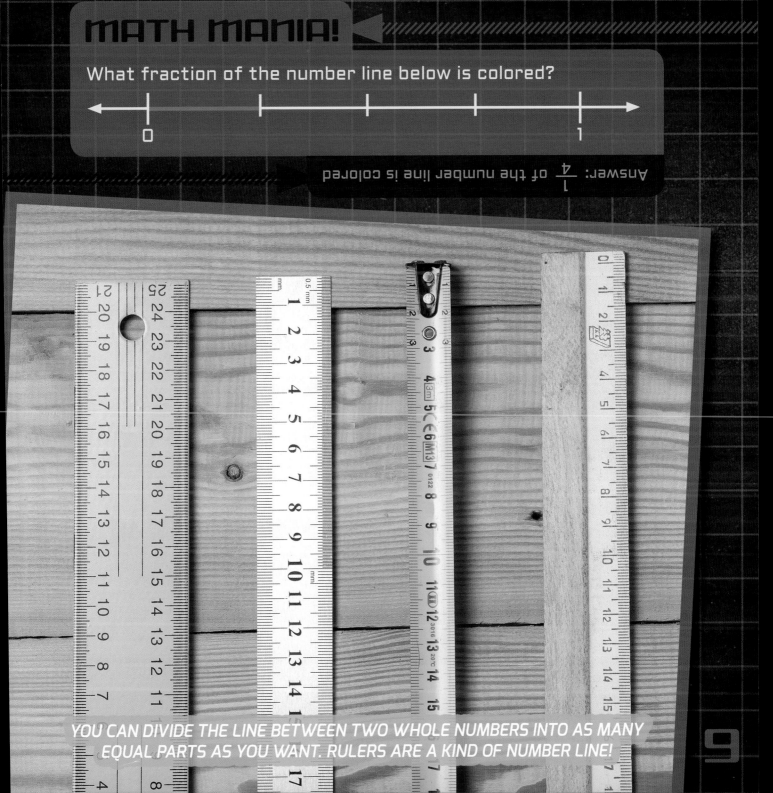

0   1

Answer: $\frac{1}{4}$ of the number line is colored

YOU CAN DIVIDE THE LINE BETWEEN TWO WHOLE NUMBERS INTO AS MANY EQUAL PARTS AS YOU WANT. RULERS ARE A KIND OF NUMBER LINE!

JUST ONE

For example, the fraction $\frac{2}{2}$ is the same as 1. You can see why in this model:

Two out of 2 blocks in the rectangle are shaded. That's the whole thing—or 1 whole rectangle.

Let's use the pizza model for the fraction $\frac{8}{8}$:

If someone ate 8 of the 8 pieces of this pizza, or $\frac{8}{8}$, they ate 1 whole pizza!

IF YOUR FRIENDS ATE 10 OF THE 10 PIECES OF THIS CAKE, THEY ATE $\frac{10}{10}$ OF THE CAKE, OR 1 WHOLE CAKE! CAN YOU NAME SOME MORE FRACTIONS THAT EQUAL 1?

MATH MANIA!

Which numbers are missing in the problems below?

a. $\frac{?}{5} = 1$ b. $\frac{8}{?} = 1$

THEY'RE THE SAME!

FAST FACT: If two or more different fractions represent the same amount, those fractions are called **equivalent**.

For example, $\frac{1}{2}$ and $\frac{2}{4}$ are equivalent. Look at the fraction models below:

$\frac{1}{2}$

$\frac{2}{4}$

The wholes are broken into different numbers of blocks, but the same amount is shaded.

You can see the same fact in the number lines below. Both fractions are halfway between 0 and 1.

0      $\frac{1}{2}$ 1

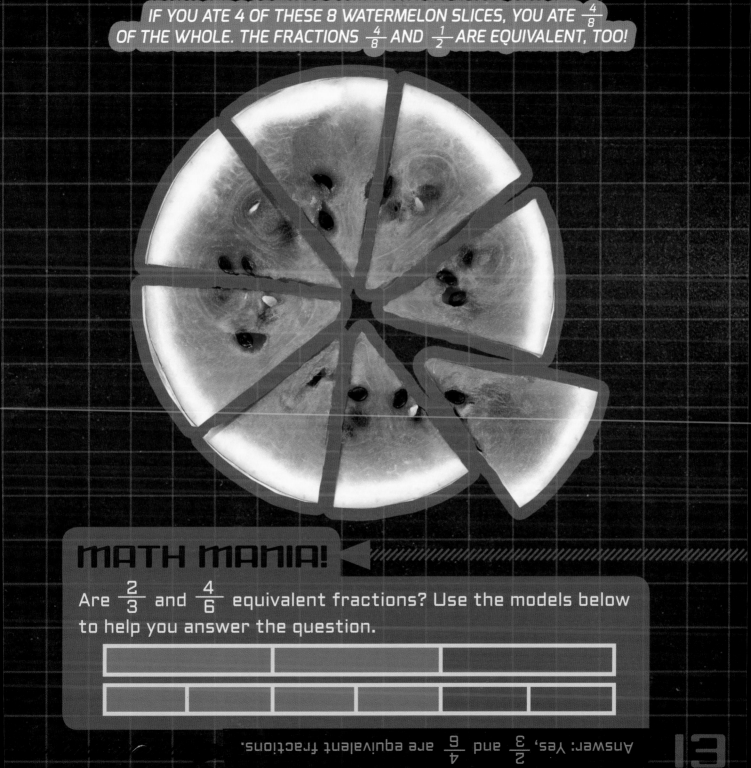

IF YOU ATE 4 OF THESE 8 WATERMELON SLICES, YOU ATE $\frac{4}{8}$ OF THE WHOLE. THE FRACTIONS $\frac{4}{8}$ AND $\frac{1}{2}$ ARE EQUIVALENT, TOO!

MATH MANIA!

Are $\frac{2}{3}$ and $\frac{4}{6}$ equivalent fractions? Use the models below to help you answer the question.

Answer: Yes, $\frac{2}{3}$ and $\frac{4}{6}$ are equivalent fractions.

IT'S NOTHING!

Let's see why this is true with pizza. If you ate $\frac{0}{3}$ pieces of this pizza, you ate none, or 0, of it:

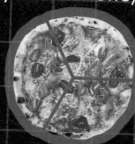

If you're told to fill in $\frac{0}{3}$ of the blocks in this model,

IMAGINE YOU HAVE 12 MARKERS. YOU USE 0 OUT OF 12 MARKERS FOR YOUR ART PROJECT, OR $\frac{0}{12}$ OF THE MARKERS. HOW MANY MARKERS DID YOU USE? NONE, OR 0!

COMPARING NUMERATORS

FAST FACT: If the denominators of two fractions are the same, the fraction with the larger numerator is the larger fraction.

Let's look at two fractions with the same denominator:

$$\frac{5}{8} \qquad \frac{7}{8}$$

The fast fact tells us that $\frac{7}{8}$ is the larger fraction. It's easy to see this using models:

$\frac{5}{8}$

$\frac{7}{8}$

FAST FACT: When one value is smaller than another, use a "less than" (<) sign to compare them. When one value is bigger than another, use a "greater than" (>) sign.

$$\frac{5}{8} < \frac{7}{8} \qquad\qquad \frac{7}{8} > \frac{5}{8}$$

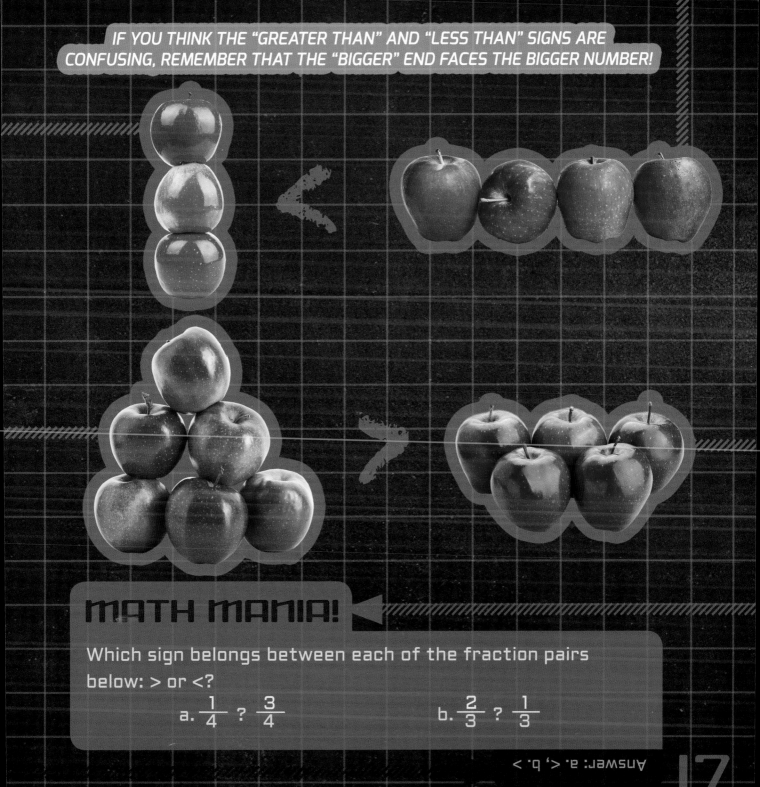

IF YOU THINK THE "GREATER THAN" AND "LESS THAN" SIGNS ARE CONFUSING, REMEMBER THAT THE "BIGGER" END FACES THE BIGGER NUMBER!

MATH MANIA!

Which sign belongs between each of the fraction pairs below: > or <?

a. $\frac{1}{4}$? $\frac{3}{4}$

b. $\frac{2}{3}$? $\frac{1}{3}$

COMPARING DENOMINATORS

In the fractions below, the numerators are the same.

The denominators are different.

$$\frac{1}{6} \ ? \ \frac{1}{4}$$

The fraction $\frac{1}{4}$ has the smaller number in the

denominator, so it's the larger fraction.

$$\frac{1}{6} < \frac{1}{4}$$

It's easy to understand this using fraction models:

$\frac{1}{6}$

$\frac{1}{4}$

HERE'S ANOTHER EXAMPLE: $\frac{5}{8}$ OF A CHOCOLATE BAR IS MORE THAN $\frac{5}{16}$ OF A CHOCOLATE BAR. FIVE PIECES OF AN OBJECT DIVIDED INTO 8 EQUAL PIECES IS A GREATER AMOUNT THAN 5 PIECES OF THE SAME OBJECT DIVIDED INTO 16 EQUAL PIECES.

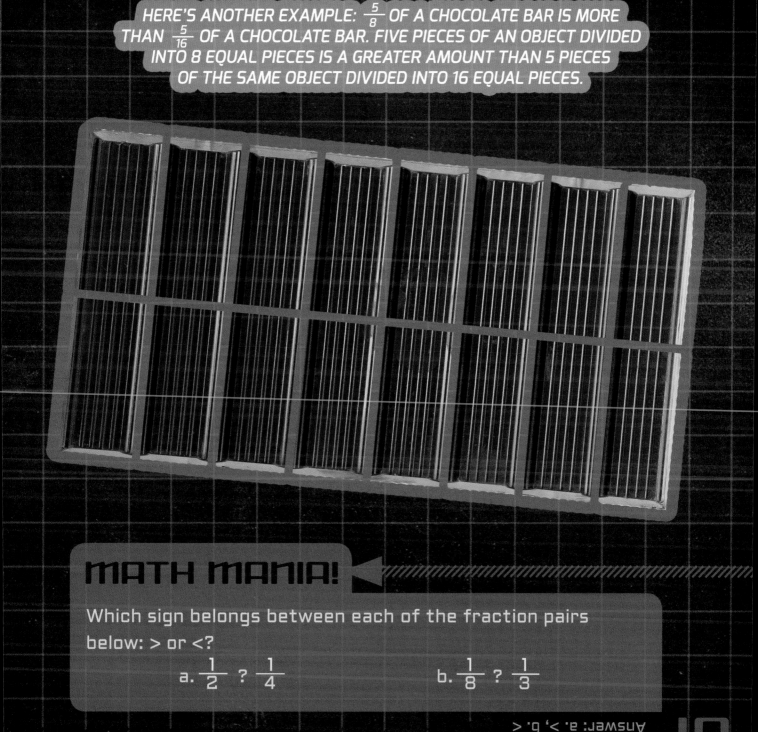

MATH MANIA!

Which sign belongs between each of the fraction pairs below: > or <?

a. $\frac{1}{2}$? $\frac{1}{4}$

b. $\frac{1}{8}$? $\frac{1}{3}$

FRACTION FANS!

So many **careers** require knowledge of fractions. Cooks use fractions when they're following **recipes**. If they didn't, the food they make might taste strange! Carpenters, **engineers**, and construction workers use fractions when they're trying to figure out certain measurements. If they didn't, the things they make might look weird—or fall over!

Now that you know more about the fractions all around you, you'll be a pro at figuring out how to use them in your life. You'll become a fraction fan!

HOW MANY FRACTIONS CAN YOU FIND IN YOUR HOME?

MATH MANIA!

Answer the fraction questions below. Review the fast facts
in this book if you have trouble.

a. In the fraction $\frac{2}{3}$, which number is the denominator?

b. Which of these three fractions are equivalent:
$$\frac{1}{2}, \frac{1}{3}, \frac{2}{4}?$$

c. Which sign belongs between the fractions below: < or >?
$$\frac{5}{6} ? \frac{1}{6}$$

d. Which sign belongs between the fractions below: < or >?
$$\frac{1}{4} ? \frac{1}{3}$$

Answer: a. 3, b. $\frac{1}{2}$ and $\frac{2}{4}$, c. >, d. <

GLOSSARY

career: a job that someone does for a long time

confusing: hard to understand

divide: to separate something into pieces

engineer: a person who plans and constructs products, machines, systems, or buildings

equivalent: having the same value, use, or meaning

mathematician: a person who is knowledgeable about mathematics

recipe: a set of steps for making food

represent: to stand for

FOR MORE INFORMATION

BOOKS

Adamson, Thomas K., and Heather Adamson. *Half You Heard of Fractions?* Mankato, MN: Capstone Press, 2012.

Kompelien, Tracy. *I Know Fractions by Their Actions!* Edina, MN: ABDO, 2007.

Pistoia, Sara, and Piper Whelan. *Fractions.* New York, NY: AV2 by Weigl, 2017.

WEBSITES

Fractions
www.mathsisfun.com/fractions.html
Read more about fractions here.

Third Grade Math
www.ixl.com/math/grade-3
Find plenty of fraction practice on this site.

23

INDEX